GIFT 99

D1460271

Contents

WITHDRAWN

Foreword

The National Curriculum lies at the heart of our policies to raise standards. It sets out a clear, full and statutory entitlement to learning for all pupils. It determines the content of what will be taught, and sets attainment targets for learning. It also determines how performance will be assessed and reported. An effective National Curriculum therefore gives teachers, pupils, parents, employers and their wider community a clear and shared understanding of the skills and knowledge that young people will gain at school. It allows schools to meet the individual learning needs of pupils and to develop a distinctive character and ethos rooted in their local communities. And it provides a framework within which all partners in education can support young people on the road to further learning.

Getting the National Curriculum right presents difficult choices and balances. It must be robust enough to define and defend the core of knowledge and cultural experience which is the entitlement of every pupil, and at the same time flexible enough to give teachers the scope to build their teaching around it in ways which will enhance its delivery to their pupils.

The focus of this National Curriculum, together with the wider school curriculum, is therefore to ensure that pupils develop from an early age the essential literacy and numeracy skills they need to learn; to provide them with a guaranteed, full and rounded entitlement to learning; to foster their creativity; and to give teachers discretion to find the best ways to inspire in their pupils a joy and commitment to learning that will last a lifetime.

An entitlement to learning must be an entitlement for all pupils. This National Curriculum includes for the first time a detailed, overarching statement on inclusion which makes clear the principles schools must follow in their teaching right across the curriculum, to ensure that all pupils have the chance to succeed, whatever their individual needs and the potential barriers to their learning may be.

Equality of opportunity is one of a broad set of common values and purposes which underpin the school curriculum and the work of schools. These also include a commitment to valuing ourselves, our families and other relationships, the wider groups to which we belong, the diversity in our society and the environment in which we live. Until now, ours was one of the few national curricula not to have a statement of rationale setting out the fundamental principles underlying the curriculum. The handbooks for primary and secondary teachers include for the first time such a statement.

This is also the first National Curriculum in England to include citizenship, from September 2002, as part of the statutory curriculum for secondary schools. Education in citizenship and democracy will provide coherence in the way in which all pupils are helped to develop a full understanding of their roles and responsibilities as citizens in a modern democracy. It will play an important role, alongside other aspects of the curriculum and school life, in helping pupils to deal with difficult moral and social questions that arise in their lives and in society. The handbooks also provide for the first time a national framework for the teaching of personal, social and health education. Both elements reflect the fact that education is also about helping pupils to develop the knowledge, skills and understanding they need to live confident, healthy, independent lives, as individuals, parents, workers and members of society

Rt Hon David Blunkett
Secretary of State for Education
and Employment

Sir William Stubbs
Chairman, Qualifications
and Curriculum Authority

About this booklet

This booklet:

- sets out the legal requirements of the National Curriculum in England for physical education
- provides information to help teachers implement physical education in their schools.

It has been written for coordinators, subject leaders and those who teach physical education, and is one of a series of separate booklets for each National Curriculum subject.

The National Curriculum for pupils aged five to 11 is set out in the handbook for primary teachers. The National Curriculum for pupils aged 11 to 16 is set out in the handbook for secondary teachers.

All these publications, and materials that support the teaching, learning and assessment of physical education, can be found on the National Curriculum web site at www.nc.uk.net.

About physical education in the National Curriculum

The structure of the National Curriculum

The programmes of study[1] set out what pupils should be taught, and the attainment target sets out the expected standards of pupils' performance. It is for schools to choose how they organise their school curriculum to include the programmes of study for physical education.

The Government believes that two hours of physical activity a week, including the National Curriculum for physical education and extra-curricular activities, should be an aspiration for all schools. This applies throughout all key stages.

Competitive games activities are compulsory throughout key stages 1 to 3. At key stage 4, although pupils can choose other activities instead of competitive team and individual games, the Government expects schools to continue to provide these for pupils who wish to take up this option.

The programmes of study

The programmes of study set out what pupils should be taught in physical education at key stages 1, 2, 3 and 4 and provide the basis for planning schemes of work. When planning, schools should also consider the general teaching requirements for inclusion, use of language, use of information and communication technology, and health and safety that apply across the programmes of study.

The **Knowledge, skills and understanding** in the programmes of study identify the aspects of physical education in which pupils make progress:

- acquiring and developing skills
- selecting and applying skills, tactics and compositional ideas
- evaluating and improving performance
- knowledge and understanding of fitness and health.

Teaching should ensure that when evaluating and improving performance, connections are made between developing, selecting and applying skills, tactics and compositional ideas, and fitness and health.

These aspects of physical education are developed through a range of activities at different key stages as set out in **Breadth of study**.

Schools may find the DfEE/QCA exemplar schemes of work at key stages 1, 2, 3 and 4 helpful to show how the programmes of study and attainment target can be translated into practical, manageable teaching plans.

[1] The Education Act 1996, section 353b, defines a programme of study as the 'matters, skills and processes' that should be taught to pupils of different abilities and maturities during the key stage.

Attainment target and level descriptions

The attainment target for physical education sets out the 'knowledge, skills and understanding that pupils of different abilities and maturities are expected to have by the end of each key stage'[2]. The attainment target consists of eight level descriptions of increasing difficulty, plus a description for exceptional performance above level 8. Each level description describes the types and range of performance that pupils working at that level should characteristically demonstrate.

In physical education, the level descriptions indicate progression in the aspects of the knowledge, skills and understanding set out in the programme of study.

The level descriptions provide the basis on which to make judgements about pupils' performance at the end of key stages 1, 2 and 3. At key stage 4, the level descriptions can be used to assess attainment and progress in physical education. National qualifications provide another means of assessing attainment in physical education.

Range of levels within which the great majority of pupils are expected to work		Expected attainment for the majority of pupils at the end of the key stage	
Key stage 1	**1–3**	at age 7	**2**
Key stage 2	**2–5**	at age 11	**4**
Key stage 3	**3–7**	at age 14	**5/6**

Assessing attainment at the end of a key stage

In deciding on a pupil's level of attainment at the end of a key stage, teachers should judge which description best fits the pupil's performance. When doing so, each description should be considered alongside descriptions for adjacent levels.

Arrangements for statutory assessment at the end of each key stage are set out in detail in QCA's annual booklets about assessment and reporting arrangements.

[2] As defined by the Education Act 1996, section 353a.

Learning across the National Curriculum

The importance of physical education to pupils' education is set out on page 15. The handbooks for primary and secondary teachers also set out in general terms how the National Curriculum can promote learning across the curriculum in a number of areas such as spiritual, moral, social and cultural development, key skills and thinking skills. The examples below indicate specific ways in which the teaching of physical education can contribute to learning across the curriculum.

Promoting pupils' spiritual, moral, social and cultural development through physical education

For example, physical education provides opportunities to promote:
- *spiritual development,* through helping pupils gain a sense of achievement and develop positive attitudes towards themselves
- *moral development,* through helping pupils gain a sense of fair play based on rules and the conventions of activities, develop positive sporting behaviour, know how to conduct themselves in sporting competitions and accept authority and support referees, umpires and judges
- *social development,* through helping pupils develop social skills in activities involving cooperation and collaboration, responsibility, personal commitment, loyalty and teamwork, and considering the social importance of physical activity, sport and dance
- *cultural development,* through helping pupils experience and understand the significance of activities from their own and other cultures [for example, folk dances and traditional games], recognise how activities and public performance gives a sense of cultural identity, and consider how sport can transcend cultural boundaries.

Promoting key skills through physical education

For example, physical education provides opportunities for pupils to develop the key skills of:
- *communication,* through promoting verbal and non-verbal communication skills when explaining what they intend to do, giving feedback to others, planning and organising group or team work, giving instructions and signals in a game, using gesture in dance, and through responding to music and other sounds in dance
- *application of number,* through collecting and analysing data [for example, to find their batting average], using different forms of measurement such as calculating the distance jumped against the percentage of their body height, understanding and using grid references and bearings in outdoor and adventurous activities, using a variety of measuring and recording equipment to take pulse, heart rates and temperatures, and using stopwatches and tapes to measure performance in running, jumping and throwing

- *IT,* through collecting, analysing and interpreting data to evaluate performance and identify priorities for improvement [for example, using video with digital tracking to analyse movement and technique, using spreadsheets to record and analyse results in athletic and swimming activities, and using databases to build their ideas, improve and record their performance]
- *working with others,* through taking on a variety of roles in groups and teams in cooperative activities, working in a group with a collective goal and deciding on strategies to meet it, cooperating with others by observing rules and conventions when competing against them
- *improving own learning and performance,* through recognising what they do well and what they need to do better, helping them to observe a good performance and to imitate it, and developing the confidence to try something new
- *problem solving,* through recognising the nature of the task or challenge, thinking of different ways to approach the task and changing their approach as the need arises, and understanding and applying the principles of movement, strategy, and composition to the task.

Promoting other aspects of the curriculum

For example, physical education provides opportunities to promote:

- *thinking skills,* through helping pupils to consider information and concepts that suit the different activities and critically evaluate aspects of performance, and to generate and express their own ideas and opinions about tactics, strategy and composition
- *work-related learning,* through helping pupils to run and organise sports and dance competitions and festivals, to take different roles including chair, secretary, treasurer, to manage and book facilities in school for pupils to use, and to assist teachers work with younger children in a variety of exercise, sport and dance clubs
- *education for sustainable development,* through developing pupils' knowledge and understanding of healthy lifestyles and of different, challenging environments.

The programmes of study for physical education

A common structure and design for all subjects

The programmes of study

The National Curriculum programmes of study have been given a common structure and a common design.

In each subject, at each key stage, the main column **1** contains the programme of study, which sets out two sorts of requirements:

- **Knowledge, skills and understanding 2** – what has to be taught in the subject during the key stage
- **Breadth of study 3** – the contexts, activities, areas of study and range of experiences through which the **Knowledge, skills and understanding** should be taught.

Schools are not required by law to teach the content in grey type. This includes the examples in the main column **4** [printed inside square brackets], all text in the margins **5** and information and examples in the inclusion statement. In the programmes of study *italic type* is used to emphasise options, where schools and teachers can choose between requirements.

The programmes of study for English, mathematics and science

The programmes of study for English and science contain sections that correspond directly to the attainment targets for each subject. In mathematics this one-to-one correspondence does not hold for all key stages – see the mathematics programme of study for more information. In English, the three sections of the programme of study each contain **Breadth of study** requirements. In mathematics and science there is a single, separate set of **Breadth of study** requirements for each key stage.

The programmes of study in the non-core foundation subjects

In these subjects (except for citizenship) the programme of study simply contains two sets of requirements – **Knowledge, skills and understanding** and **Breadth of study**. The programmes of study for citizenship contain no **Breadth of study** requirements.

Information in the margins

At the start of each key stage, the margin begins with a summary **6** of the main things that pupils will learn during the key stage. The margins also contain four other types of non-statutory information:

- notes giving key information that should be taken into account when teaching the subject
- notes giving definitions of words and phrases in the programmes of study
- suggested opportunities for pupils to use information and communication technology (ICT) as they learn the subject
- some key links with other subjects indicating connections between teaching requirements, and suggesting how a requirement in one subject can build on the requirements in another in the same key stage.

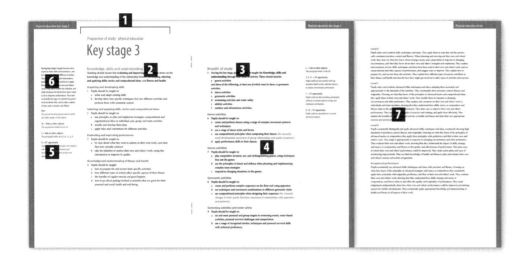

The referencing system

References work as follows:

A reference in …	… reads …	… and means …
Physical education key stage 2	**11a, 11b → links to other subjects** These requirements build on Gg/2c.	Physical education key stage 2, requirements 11a and 11b build on geography (key stage 2), paragraph 2, requirement c.
Art and design key stage 1	**4a → links to other subjects** This requirement builds on Ma3/2a, 2c, 2d.	Art and design key stage 1, requirement 4a builds on mathematics (key stage 1), Ma3 Shape, space and measures, paragraph 2, requirements a, c and d.
Citizenship key stage 3	**1a → links to other subjects** This requirement builds on Hi/10, 13.	Citizenship key stage 3, requirement 1a builds on history (key stage 3) paragraphs 10 and 13.

The attainment target

The attainment target **7** is at the end of this booklet. It can be read alongside the programmes of study by folding out the flap.

PE Makes heart

To see young people growing in
physical skills, self-confidence and
self-worth is a truly enriching
experience. Nowhere in school
is it more visible than in PE.

Duncan Goodhew, Swimmer

Exercise activates your brain and
gives you energy for everything else,
the energy to be enthusiastic about
your work. So all your school work
will gain from physical education.

Darcey Bussell, Dancer, The Royal Ballet

Physical education is about pupils
learning about themselves: their
capabilities, their potential and their
limitations. It is the foundation
of all sports participation. But it
goes beyond the individual and
understanding themselves – it's
learning how to work with and
to respect others.

Lucy Pearson, England Cricketer and Teacher

your

beat

faster.

The importance of physical education

Physical education develops pupils' physical competence and confidence, and their ability to use these to perform in a range of activities. It promotes physical skillfulness, physical development and a knowledge of the body in action. Physical education provides opportunities for pupils to be creative, competitive and to face up to different challenges as individuals and in groups and teams. It promotes positive attitudes towards active and healthy lifestyles.

Pupils learn how to think in different ways to suit a wide variety of creative, competitive and challenging activities. They learn how to plan, perform and evaluate actions, ideas and performances to improve their quality and effectiveness. Through this process pupils discover their aptitudes, abilities and preferences, and make choices about how to get involved in lifelong physical activity.

Programme of study: physical education

Key stage 1

During key stage 1 pupils build on their
natural enthusiasm for movement, using
it to explore and learn about their world.
They start to work and play with other
pupils in pairs and small groups.
By watching, listening and experimenting,
they develop their skills in movement
and coordination, and enjoy expressing
and testing themselves in a variety
of situations.

Note
The general teaching requirement for health
and safety applies in this subject.

3a → links to other subjects
This requirement builds on En1/1.

4 → links to other subjects
These requirements build on Sc2/2c.

Knowledge, skills and understanding
Teaching should ensure that when **evaluating and improving performance**,
connections are made between **developing, selecting and applying skills,
tactics and compositional ideas**, and **fitness and health**.

Acquiring and developing skills
1 Pupils should be taught to:
   a explore basic skills, actions and ideas with increasing understanding
   b remember and repeat simple skills and actions with increasing control
      and coordination.

Selecting and applying skills, tactics and compositional ideas
2 Pupils should be taught to:
   a explore how to choose and apply skills and actions in sequence and
      in combination
   b vary the way they perform skills by using simple tactics and movement phrases
   c apply rules and conventions for different activities.

Evaluating and improving performance
3 Pupils should be taught to:
   a describe what they have done
   b observe, describe and copy what others have done
   c use what they have learnt to improve the quality and control of their work.

Knowledge and understanding of fitness and health
4 Pupils should be taught:
   a how important it is to be active
   b to recognise and describe how their bodies feel during different activities.

Breadth of study

5   During the key stage, pupils should be taught the **Knowledge, skills and understanding** through dance activities, games activities and gymnastic activities.

Dance activities

6   Pupils should be taught to:

a   use movement imaginatively, responding to stimuli, including music, and performing basic skills [for example, travelling, being still, making a shape, jumping, turning and gesturing]

b   change the rhythm, speed, level and direction of their movements

c   create and perform dances using simple movement patterns, including those from different times and cultures

d   express and communicate ideas and feelings.

Games activities

7   Pupils should be taught to:

a   travel with, send and receive a ball and other equipment in different ways

b   develop these skills for simple net, striking/fielding and invasion-type games

c   play simple, competitive net, striking/fielding and invasion-type games that they and others have made, using simple tactics for attacking and defending.

Gymnastic activities

8   Pupils should be taught to:

a   perform basic skills in travelling, being still, finding space and using it safely, both on the floor and using apparatus

b   develop the range of their skills and actions [for example, balancing, taking off and landing, turning and rolling]

c   choose and link skills and actions in short movement phrases

d   create and perform short, linked sequences that show a clear beginning, middle and end and have contrasts in direction, level and speed.

The following are non-statutory guidelines.

Swimming activities and water safety

9   Pupils should be taught to:

a   move in water [for example, jump, walk, hop and spin, using swimming aids and support]

b   float and move with and without swimming aids

c   feel the buoyancy and support of water and swimming aids

d   propel themselves in water using different swimming aids, arm and leg actions and basic strokes.

---

6 → links to other subjects
These requirements build on Mu/3a, 4d, 5b.

6, 8 → ICT opportunity
Pupils could use videos of movements and actions to develop their ideas.

8 → ICT opportunity
Pupils could use a concept keyboard to record the order of specific actions in their sequences.

Note for 9
Schools can also choose to teach swimming during key stage 1. Paragraph 9 gives non-statutory guidelines, which identify aspects of swimming activities and water safety appropriate for key stage 1 pupils.

Programme of study: physical education

Key stage 2

During key stage 2 pupils enjoy being active and using their creativity and imagination in physical activity. They learn new skills, find out how to use them in different ways, and link them to make actions, phrases and sequences of movement. They enjoy communicating, collaborating and competing with each other. They develop an understanding of how to succeed in different activities and learn how to evaluate and recognise their own success.

Note
The general teaching requirement for health and safety applies in this subject.

3b → links to other subjects
This requirement builds on En1/3b.

4 → links to other subjects
These requirements build on Sc2/2c–2e, 2h.

Knowledge, skills and understanding
Teaching should ensure that when **evaluating and improving performance**, connections are made between **developing, selecting and applying skills, tactics and compositional ideas**, and **fitness and health**.

Acquiring and developing skills
1   Pupils should be taught to:
   a   consolidate their existing skills and gain new ones
   b   perform actions and skills with more consistent control and quality.

Selecting and applying skills, tactics and compositional ideas
2   Pupils should be taught to:
   a   plan, use and adapt strategies, tactics and compositional ideas for individual, pair, small-group and small-team activities
   b   develop and use their knowledge of the principles behind the strategies, tactics and ideas to improve their effectiveness
   c   apply rules and conventions for different activities.

Evaluating and improving performance
3   Pupils should be taught to:
   a   identify what makes a performance effective
   b   suggest improvements based on this information.

Knowledge and understanding of fitness and health
4   Pupils should be taught:
   a   how exercise affects the body in the short term
   b   to warm up and prepare appropriately for different activities
   c   why physical activity is good for their health and well-being
   d   why wearing appropriate clothing and being hygienic is good for their health and safety.

Breadth of study
5   During the key stage, pupils should be taught the **Knowledge, skills and understanding** through five areas of activity:
   a   dance activities
   b   games activities
   c   gymnastic activities
   and two activity areas from:
   d   swimming activities and water safety
   e   athletic activities
   f   outdoor and adventurous activities.
   Swimming activities and water safety must be chosen as one of these areas of activity unless pupils have completed the full key stage 2 teaching requirements in relation to swimming activities and water safety during key stage 1.

Dance activities

6 Pupils should be taught to:

a create and perform dances using a range of movement patterns, including those from different times, places and cultures

b respond to a range of stimuli and accompaniment.

Games activities

7 Pupils should be taught to:

a play and make up small-sided and modified competitive net, striking/fielding and invasion games

b use skills and tactics and apply basic principles suitable for attacking and defending

c work with others to organise and keep the games going.

Gymnastic activities

8 Pupils should be taught to:

a create and perform fluent sequences on the floor and using apparatus

b include variations in level, speed and direction in their sequences.

Swimming activities and water safety

9 Pupils should be taught to:

a pace themselves in floating and swimming challenges related to speed, distance and personal survival

b swim unaided for a sustained period of time over a distance of at least 25m

c use recognised arm and leg actions, lying on their front and back

d use a range of recognised strokes and personal survival skills [for example, front crawl, back crawl, breaststroke, sculling, floating and surface diving]

Athletic activities

10 Pupils should be taught to:

a take part in and design challenges and competitions that call for precision, speed, power or stamina

b use running, jumping and throwing skills both singly and in combination

c pace themselves in these challenges and competitions.

Outdoor and adventurous activities

11 Pupils should be taught to:

a take part in outdoor activity challenges, including following trails, in familiar, unfamiliar and changing environments

b use a range of orienteering and problem-solving skills

c work with others to meet the challenges.

6 → links to other subjects
These requirements build on Mu/3b, 5b.

6, 8 → ICT opportunity
Pupils could use video recordings of their sequences and dances to compare ideas and quality.

6, 8, 10 → ICT opportunity
Pupils could use video and CD-ROMs of actions, balances and body shapes to improve their performance.

Note for 9
If aspects of swimming and water safety have been taught during key stage 1, pupils should start this area of activity at the appropriate point.

11a, 11b → links to other subjects
These requirements build on Gg/2c.

During key stage 3 pupils become more expert in their skills and techniques, and how to apply them in different activities. They start to understand what makes a performance effective and how to apply these principles to their own and others' work. They learn to take the initiative and make decisions for themselves about what to do to improve performance. They start to identify the types of activity they prefer to be involved with, and to take a variety of roles such as leader and official.

Note
The general teaching requirement for health and safety applies in this subject.

3b → links to other subjects
This requirement builds on En1/3e.

4 → links to other subjects
These requirements build on Sc2/2e, 2i, 2j, 2l.

4 → ICT opportunity
Pupils could use heart and pulse rate monitors and a variety of other measuring and recording devices to collect, analyse and interpret data.

Programme of study: physical education

Key stage 3

Knowledge, skills and understanding

Teaching should ensure that, when **evaluating and improving performance**, connections are made between **developing, selecting and applying skills, tactics and compositional ideas**, and **fitness and health**.

Acquiring and developing skills
1   Pupils should be taught to:
   a   refine and adapt existing skills
   b   develop them into specific techniques that suit different activities and perform these with consistent control.

Selecting and applying skills, tactics and compositional ideas
2   Pupils should be taught to:
   a   use principles to plan and implement strategies, compositional and organisational ideas in individual, pair, group and team activities
   b   modify and develop their plans
   c   apply rules and conventions for different activities.

Evaluating and improving performance
3   Pupils should be taught to:
   a   be clear about what they want to achieve in their own work, and what they have actually achieved
   b   take the initiative to analyse their own and others' work, using this information to improve its quality.

Knowledge and understanding of fitness and health
4   Pupils should be taught:
   a   how to prepare for and recover from specific activities
   b   how different types of activity affect specific aspects of their fitness
   c   the benefits of regular exercise and good hygiene
   d   how to go about getting involved in activities that are good for their personal and social health and well-being.

Breadth of study

5 During the key stage, pupils should be taught the **Knowledge, skills and understanding** through four areas of activity. These should include:

  a games activities

  and three of the following, *at least one of which must be dance or gymnastic activities:*

  b dance activities

  c gymnastic activities

  d swimming activities and water safety

  e athletic activities

  f outdoor and adventurous activities.

Dance activities

6 Pupils should be taught to:

  a create and perform dances using a range of complex movement patterns and techniques

  b use a range of dance styles and forms

  c use compositional principles when composing their dances [for example, motif development, awareness of group relationships, spatial awareness]

  d apply performance skills in their dances.

Games activities

7 Pupils should be taught to:

  a play competitive invasion, net and striking/fielding games, using techniques that suit the games

  b use the principles of attack and defence when planning and implementing complex team strategies

  c respond to changing situations in the games.

Gymnastic activities

8 Pupils should be taught to:

  a create and perform complex sequences on the floor and using apparatus

  b use techniques and movement combinations in different gymnastic styles

  c use compositional principles when designing their sequences [for example, changes in level, speed, direction, and relationships with apparatus and partners].

Swimming activities and water safety

9 Pupils should be taught to:

  a set and meet personal and group targets in swimming events, water-based activities, personal survival challenges and competitions

  b use a range of recognised strokes, techniques and personal survival skills with technical proficiency.

---

6 → links to other subjects
These requirements build on Mu/2b.

7 → ICT opportunity
Pupils could use data-recording and analysis software to analyse patterns of play and individual contributions.

7, 9–11 → ICT opportunity
Pupils could use stop watches with lap recorders linked to data-collection devices to analyse and evaluate performance.

9, 10 → ICT opportunity
Pupils could use spreadsheets to record and track progress.

11b → links to other subjects
This requirement builds on Gg/2c.

Athletic activities

10 Pupils should be taught to:

a set and meet personal and group targets in a range of athletic events, challenges and competitions

b use a range of running, jumping and throwing techniques, singly and in combination, with precision, speed, power or stamina.

Outdoor and adventurous activities

11 Pupils should be taught to:

a meet challenges in outdoor activities and journeys

b use a range of orienteering and problem-solving skills and techniques in these challenges

c identify the roles and responsibilities of individuals within a group when planning strategies

d respond to changing conditions and situations.

Programme of study: physical education

Key stage 4

Knowledge, skills and understanding

Teaching should ensure that, when **evaluating and improving performance**, connections are made between **developing, selecting and applying skills, tactics and compositional ideas**, and **fitness and health**.

Acquiring and developing skills

1   Pupils should be taught to:
   a   develop and apply advanced skills and techniques
   b   apply them in increasingly demanding situations.

Selecting and applying skills, tactics and compositional ideas

2   Pupils should be taught to:
   a   use advanced strategic and/or choreographic and organisational concepts and principles
   b   apply these concepts and principles in increasingly demanding situations
   c   apply rules and conventions for different activities.

Evaluating and improving performance

3   Pupils should be taught to:
   a   make informed choices about what role they want to take in each activity
   b   judge how good a performance is and decide how to improve it
   c   prioritise and carry out these decisions to improve their own and others' performances
   d   develop leadership skills.

Knowledge and understanding of fitness and health

4   Pupils should be taught:
   a   how preparation, training and fitness relate to and affect performance
   b   how to design and carry out activity and training programmes that have specific purposes
   c   the importance of exercise and activity to personal, social and mental health and well-being
   d   how to monitor and develop their own training, exercise and activity programmes in and out of school.

During key stage 4 pupils tackle complex and demanding activities applying their knowledge of skills, techniques and effective performance. They decide whether to get involved in physical activity that is mainly focused on competing or performing, promoting health and well-being, or developing personal fitness. They also decide on roles that suit them best including performer, coach, choreographer, leader and official. The view they have of their skillfulness and physical competence gives them the confidence to get involved in exercise and activity out of school and in later life.

Note
The general teaching requirement for health and safety applies in this subject.

3 → links to other subjects
These requirements build on En1/3a–3e.

4 → links to other subjects
These requirements build on Sc2/2e, 2f (double).

6 → ICT opportunity
Pupils could use multimedia devices to create sounds and music and provide lighting and other effects to enhance their dance.

6, 8, 10 → ICT opportunity
Pupils could use databases of movement ideas and techniques to analyse and evaluate performance.

6, 8–10 → ICT opportunity
Pupils could use digital cameras to help them to analyse actions and techniques.

7 → ICT opportunity
Pupils could use videos of games analysis to develop understanding of patterns of play and individual contributions.

9–11 → ICT opportunity
Pupils could use a variety of electronic and digital recording, measuring and timing devices to measure the effectiveness of performance.

9, 10 → ICT opportunity
Pupils could use spreadsheets to collect, analyse and interpret data.

Breadth of study

5   During the key stage, pupils should be taught the **Knowledge, skills and understanding** through *two of the six activity areas*.

Dance activities

6   Pupils should be taught to:
a   choreograph and perform complex dances using advanced techniques and skills with accuracy and expression
b   reflect different social and cultural contexts in their dances and communicate artistic intention
c   use presentational skills in their dances.

Games activities

7   Pupils should be taught to:
a   play competitive games
b   use advanced techniques and skills specific to the games played with consistency and control
c   respond effectively to changing situations within their games.

Gymnastic activities

8   Pupils should be taught to:
a   compose and perform sequences, both on the floor and using apparatus, in specific gymnastic styles, applying set criteria
b   use advanced techniques and skills with precision and accuracy
c   use advanced compositional concepts and principles when composing their sequences.

Swimming activities and water safety

9   Pupils should be taught to:
a   meet challenges in specific swimming events and water-based activities
b   use advanced techniques and skills with control, power or stamina and technical proficiency.

Athletic activities

10 Pupils should be taught to:
a   take part in specific athletic events
b   use advanced techniques and skills with precision, speed, power or stamina and technical proficiency.

Outdoor and adventurous activities

11 Pupils should be taught to:

a   meet challenges in large-scale outdoor activities and journeys

b   use a range of complex outdoor activity skills and techniques [for example, canoeing, sailing, rock climbing, hillwalking]

c   solve problems and overcome challenges in unfamiliar environments

d   respond to changing conditions and environments.

General teaching requirements

Inclusion: providing effective learning opportunities for all pupils

Schools have a responsibility to provide a broad and balanced curriculum for all pupils. The National Curriculum is the starting point for planning a school curriculum that meets the specific needs of individuals and groups of pupils. This statutory inclusion statement on providing effective learning opportunities for all pupils outlines how teachers can modify, as necessary, the National Curriculum programmes of study to provide all pupils with relevant and appropriately challenging work at each key stage. It sets out three principles that are essential to developing a more inclusive curriculum:

A Setting suitable learning challenges

B Responding to pupils' diverse learning needs

C Overcoming potential barriers to learning and assessment for individuals and groups of pupils.

Applying these principles should keep to a minimum the need for aspects of the National Curriculum to be disapplied for a pupil.

Schools are able to provide other curricular opportunities outside the National Curriculum to meet the needs of individuals or groups of pupils such as speech and language therapy and mobility training.

Three principles for inclusion

In planning and teaching the National Curriculum, teachers are required to have due regard to the following principles.

A Setting suitable learning challenges

1 Teachers should aim to give every pupil the opportunity to experience success in learning and to achieve as high a standard as possible. The National Curriculum programmes of study set out what most pupils should be taught at each key stage – but teachers should teach the knowledge, skills and understanding in ways that suit their pupils' abilities. This may mean choosing knowledge, skills and understanding from earlier or later key stages so that individual pupils can make progress and show what they can achieve. Where it is appropriate for pupils to make extensive use of content from an earlier key stage, there may not be time to teach all aspects of the age-related programmes of study. A similarly flexible approach will be needed to take account of any gaps in pupils' learning resulting from missed or interrupted schooling [for example, that may be experienced by travellers, refugees, those in care or those with long-term medical conditions, including pupils with neurological problems, such as head injuries, and those with degenerative conditions].

2   For pupils whose attainments fall significantly below the expected levels at
    a particular key stage, a much greater degree of differentiation will be necessary.
    In these circumstances, teachers may need to use the content of the programmes
    of study as a resource or to provide a context, in planning learning appropriate
    to the age and requirements of their pupils.[1]

3   For pupils whose attainments significantly exceed the expected level of
    attainment within one or more subjects during a particular key stage, teachers
    will need to plan suitably challenging work. As well as drawing on materials
    from later key stages or higher levels of study, teachers may plan further
    differentiation by extending the breadth and depth of study within individual
    subjects or by planning work which draws on the content of different subjects.[2]

B   Responding to pupils' diverse learning needs

1   When planning, teachers should set high expectations and provide
    opportunities for all pupils to achieve, including boys and girls, pupils with
    special educational needs, pupils with disabilities, pupils from all social and
    cultural backgrounds, pupils of different ethnic groups including travellers,
    refugees and asylum seekers, and those from diverse linguistic backgrounds.
    Teachers need to be aware that pupils bring to school different experiences,
    interests and strengths which will influence the way in which they learn.
    Teachers should plan their approaches to teaching and learning so that all
    pupils can take part in lessons fully and effectively.

2   To ensure that they meet the full range of pupils' needs, teachers should be
    aware of the requirements of the equal opportunities legislation that covers
    race, gender and disability.[3]

3   Teachers should take specific action to respond to pupils' diverse needs by:
    a   creating effective learning environments
    b   securing their motivation and concentration
    c   providing equality of opportunity through teaching approaches
    d   using appropriate assessment approaches
    e   setting targets for learning.

Examples for B/3a – creating effective learning environments
Teachers create effective learning environments in which:
- the contribution of all pupils is valued
- all pupils can feel secure and are able to contribute appropriately
- stereotypical views are challenged and pupils learn to appreciate and view
  positively differences in others, whether arising from race, gender, ability
  or disability

[1] Teachers may find QCA's guidance on planning work for pupils with learning difficulties a helpful
    companion to the programmes of study.
[2] Teachers may find QCA's guidance on meeting the requirements of gifted and talented pupils
    a helpful companion to the programmes of study.
[3] The Sex Discrimination Act 1975, the Race Relations Act 1976, the Disability Discrimination Act 1995.

- pupils learn to take responsibility for their actions and behaviours both in school and in the wider community
- all forms of bullying and harassment, including racial harassment, are challenged
- pupils are enabled to participate safely in clothing appropriate to their religious beliefs, particularly in subjects such as science, design and technology and physical education.

Examples for B/3b – securing motivation and concentration

Teachers secure pupils' motivation and concentration by:

- using teaching approaches appropriate to different learning styles
- using, where appropriate, a range of organisational approaches, such as setting, grouping or individual work, to ensure that learning needs are properly addressed
- varying subject content and presentation so that this matches their learning needs
- planning work which builds on their interests and cultural experiences
- planning appropriately challenging work for those whose ability and understanding are in advance of their language skills
- using materials which reflect social and cultural diversity and provide positive images of race, gender and disability
- planning and monitoring the pace of work so that they all have a chance to learn effectively and achieve success
- taking action to maintain interest and continuity of learning for pupils who may be absent for extended periods of time.

Examples for B/3c – providing equality of opportunity

Teaching approaches that provide equality of opportunity include:

- ensuring that boys and girls are able to participate in the same curriculum, particularly in science, design and technology and physical education
- taking account of the interests and concerns of boys and girls by using a range of activities and contexts for work and allowing a variety of interpretations and outcomes, particularly in English, science, design and technology, ICT, art and design, music and physical education
- avoiding gender stereotyping when organising pupils into groups, assigning them to activities or arranging access to equipment, particularly in science, design and technology, ICT, music and physical education
- taking account of pupils' specific religious or cultural beliefs relating to the representation of ideas or experiences or to the use of particular types of equipment, particularly in science, design and technology, ICT and art and design
- enabling the fullest possible participation of pupils with disabilities or particular medical needs in all subjects, offering positive role models and making provision, where necessary, to facilitate access to activities with appropriate support, aids or adaptations. (See **Overcoming potential barriers to learning and assessment for individuals and groups of pupils.**)

Examples for B/3d – using appropriate assessment approaches

Teachers use appropriate assessment approaches that:

- allow for different learning styles and ensure that pupils are given the chance and encouragement to demonstrate their competence and attainment through appropriate means
- are familiar to the pupils and for which they have been adequately prepared
- use materials which are free from discrimination and stereotyping in any form
- provide clear and unambiguous feedback to pupils to aid further learning.

Examples for B/3e – setting targets for learning

Teachers set targets for learning that:

- build on pupils' knowledge, experiences, interests and strengths to improve areas of weakness and demonstrate progression over time
- are attainable and yet challenging and help pupils to develop their self-esteem and confidence in their ability to learn.

C Overcoming potential barriers to learning and assessment for individuals and groups of pupils

A minority of pupils will have particular learning and assessment requirements which go beyond the provisions described in sections A and B and, if not addressed, could create barriers to learning. These requirements are likely to arise as a consequence of a pupil having a special educational need or disability or may be linked to a pupil's progress in learning English as an additional language.

1   Teachers must take account of these requirements and make provision, where necessary, to support individuals or groups of pupils to enable them to participate effectively in the curriculum and assessment activities. During end of key stage assessments, teachers should bear in mind that special arrangements are available to support individual pupils.

Pupils with special educational needs

2   Curriculum planning and assessment for pupils with special educational needs must take account of the type and extent of the difficulty experienced by the pupil. Teachers will encounter a wide range of pupils with special educational needs, some of whom will also have disabilities (see paragraphs C/4 and C/5). In many cases, the action necessary to respond to an individual's requirements for curriculum access will be met through greater differentiation of tasks and materials, consistent with school-based intervention as set out in the SEN Code of Practice. A smaller number of pupils may need access to specialist equipment and approaches or to alternative or adapted activities, consistent with school-based intervention augmented by advice and support from external specialists as described in the SEN Code of Practice, or, in exceptional circumstances, with a statement of special educational need.

Teachers should, where appropriate, work closely with representatives of other agencies who may be supporting the pupil.

3   Teachers should take specific action to provide access to learning for pupils with special educational needs by:
   a   providing for pupils who need help with communication, language and literacy
   b   planning, where necessary, to develop pupils' understanding through the use of all available senses and experiences
   c   planning for pupils' full participation in learning and in physical and practical activities
   d   helping pupils to manage their behaviour, to take part in learning effectively and safely, and, at key stage 4, to prepare for work
   e   helping individuals to manage their emotions, particularly trauma or stress, and to take part in learning.

Examples for C/3a – helping with communication, language and literacy
Teachers provide for pupils who need help with communication, language and literacy through:
- using texts that pupils can read and understand
- using visual and written materials in different formats, including large print, symbol text and Braille
- using ICT, other technological aids and taped materials
- using alternative and augmentative communication, including signs and symbols
- using translators, communicators and amanuenses.

Examples for C/3b – developing understanding
Teachers develop pupils' understanding through the use of all available senses and experiences, by:
- using materials and resources that pupils can access through sight, touch, sound, taste or smell
- using word descriptions and other stimuli to make up for a lack of first-hand experiences
- using ICT, visual and other materials to increase pupils' knowledge of the wider world
- encouraging pupils to take part in everyday activities such as play, drama, class visits and exploring the environment.

Examples for C/3c – planning for full participation
Teachers plan for pupils' full participation in learning and in physical and practical activities through:
- using specialist aids and equipment
- providing support from adults or peers when needed
- adapting tasks or environments
- providing alternative activities, where necessary.

Examples for C/3d – managing behaviour

Teachers help pupils to manage their behaviour, take part in learning effectively and safely, and, at key stage 4, prepare for work by:

- setting realistic demands and stating them explicitly
- using positive behaviour management, including a clear structure of rewards and sanctions
- giving pupils every chance and encouragement to develop the skills they need to work well with a partner or a group
- teaching pupils to value and respect the contribution of others
- encouraging and teaching independent working skills
- teaching essential safety rules.

Examples for C/3e – managing emotions

Teachers help individuals manage their emotions and take part in learning through:

- identifying aspects of learning in which the pupil will engage and plan short-term, easily achievable goals in selected activities
- providing positive feedback to reinforce and encourage learning and build self-esteem
- selecting tasks and materials sensitively to avoid unnecessary stress for the pupil
- creating a supportive learning environment in which the pupil feels safe and is able to engage with learning
- allowing time for the pupil to engage with learning and gradually increasing the range of activities and demands.

Pupils with disabilities

4   Not all pupils with disabilities will necessarily have special educational needs. Many pupils with disabilities learn alongside their peers with little need for additional resources beyond the aids which they use as part of their daily life, such as a wheelchair, a hearing aid or equipment to aid vision. Teachers must take action, however, in their planning to ensure that these pupils are enabled to participate as fully and effectively as possible within the National Curriculum and the statutory assessment arrangements. Potential areas of difficulty should be identified and addressed at the outset of work, without recourse to the formal provisions for disapplication.

5   Teachers should take specific action to enable the effective participation of pupils with disabilities by:
   a   planning appropriate amounts of time to allow for the satisfactory completion of tasks
   b   planning opportunities, where necessary, for the development of skills in practical aspects of the curriculum
   c   identifying aspects of programmes of study and attainment targets that may present specific difficulties for individuals.

Examples for C/5a – planning to complete tasks

Teachers plan appropriate amounts of time to allow pupils to complete tasks satisfactorily through:

- taking account of the very slow pace at which some pupils will be able to record work, either manually or with specialist equipment, and of the physical effort required
- being aware of the high levels of concentration necessary for some pupils when following or interpreting text or graphics, particularly when using vision aids or tactile methods, and of the tiredness which may result
- allocating sufficient time, opportunity and access to equipment for pupils to gain information through experimental work and detailed observation, including the use of microscopes
- being aware of the effort required by some pupils to follow oral work, whether through use of residual hearing, lip reading or a signer, and of the tiredness or loss of concentration which may occur.

Examples for C/5b – developing skills in practical aspects

Teachers create opportunities for the development of skills in practical aspects of the curriculum through:

- providing adapted, modified or alternative activities or approaches to learning in physical education and ensuring that these have integrity and equivalence to the National Curriculum and enable pupils to make appropriate progress
- providing alternative or adapted activities in science, art and design and design and technology for pupils who are unable to manipulate tools, equipment or materials or who may be allergic to certain types of materials
- ensuring that all pupils can be included and participate safely in geography fieldwork, local studies and visits to museums, historic buildings and sites.

Examples for C/5c – overcoming specific difficulties

Teachers overcome specific difficulties for individuals presented by aspects of the programmes of study and attainment targets through:

- using approaches to enable hearing impaired pupils to learn about sound in science and music
- helping visually impaired pupils to learn about light in science, to access maps and visual resources in geography and to evaluate different products in design and technology and images in art and design
- providing opportunities for pupils to develop strength in depth where they cannot meet the particular requirements of a subject, such as the visual requirements in art and design and the singing requirements in music
- discounting these aspects in appropriate individual cases when required to make a judgement against level descriptions.

Pupils who are learning English as an additional language

6   Pupils for whom English is an additional language have diverse needs in terms of support necessary in English language learning. Planning should take account of such factors as the pupil's age, length of time in this country, previous educational experience and skills in other languages. Careful monitoring of each pupil's progress in the acquisition of English language skills and of subject knowledge and understanding will be necessary to confirm that no learning difficulties are present.

7   The ability of pupils for whom English is an additional language to take part in the National Curriculum may be ahead of their communication skills in English. Teachers should plan learning opportunities to help pupils develop their English and should aim to provide the support pupils need to take part in all subject areas.

8   Teachers should take specific action to help pupils who are learning English as an additional language by:
    a   developing their spoken and written English
    b   ensuring access to the curriculum and to assessment.

Examples for C/8a – developing spoken and written English

Teachers develop pupils' spoken and written English through:

- ensuring that vocabulary work covers both the technical and everyday meaning of key words, metaphors and idioms
- explaining clearly how speaking and writing in English are structured to achieve different purposes, across a range of subjects
- providing a variety of reading material [for example, pupils' own work, the media, ICT, literature, reference books] that highlight the different ways English is used, especially those that help pupils to understand society and culture
- ensuring that there are effective opportunities for talk and that talk is used to support writing in all subjects
- where appropriate, encouraging pupils to transfer their knowledge, skills and understanding of one language to another, pointing out similarities and differences between languages
- building on pupils' experiences of language at home and in the wider community, so that their developing uses of English and other languages support one another.

Examples for C/8b – ensuring access

Teachers make sure pupils have access to the curriculum and to assessment through:

- using accessible texts and materials that suit pupils' ages and levels of learning
- providing support by using ICT or video or audio materials, dictionaries and translators, readers and amanuenses
- using home or first language, where appropriate.

Additional information for physical education

Teachers may find the following additional information helpful when implementing the statutory inclusion statement: **Providing effective learning opportunities for all pupils.** Teachers need to consider the full requirements of the inclusion statement when planning for individuals or groups of pupils. There are specific references to physical education in the examples for B/3a, B/3c and C/5b. Teachers also need to take account of pupils' religious and cultural beliefs and practices through providing appropriate physical activity and opportunities for learning at times of fasting.

To overcome any potential barriers to learning in physical education some pupils may require:

- adapted, modified or alternative activities that have integrity and equivalence to the activities in the programmes of study and that enable the pupils to make progress
- specific support to enable them to participate in certain activities or types of movement
- careful management of their physical regime to allow for specific medical conditions.

In assessment:

- when pupils follow adapted or alternative activities, judgements against level descriptions should be made in the context of the activities undertaken by the pupil.

Use of language across the curriculum

1 Pupils should be taught in all subjects to express themselves correctly and appropriately and to read accurately and with understanding. Since standard English, spoken and written, is the predominant language in which knowledge and skills are taught and learned, pupils should be taught to recognise and use standard English.

Writing

2 In writing, pupils should be taught to use correct spelling and punctuation and follow grammatical conventions. They should also be taught to organise their writing in logical and coherent forms.

Speaking

3 In speaking, pupils should be taught to use language precisely and cogently.

Listening

4 Pupils should be taught to listen to others, and to respond and build on their ideas and views constructively.

Reading

5 In reading, pupils should be taught strategies to help them read with understanding, to locate and use information, to follow a process or argument and summarise, and to synthesise and adapt what they learn from their reading.

6 Pupils should be taught the technical and specialist vocabulary of subjects and how to use and spell these words. They should also be taught to use the patterns of language vital to understanding and expression in different subjects. These include the construction of sentences, paragraphs and texts that are often used in a subject [for example, language to express causality, chronology, logic, exploration, hypothesis, comparison, and how to ask questions and develop arguments].

Use of information and communication technology across the curriculum

1 Pupils should be given opportunities[1] to apply and develop their ICT capability through the use of ICT tools to support their learning in all subjects (with the exception of physical education at key stages 1 and 2).

2 Pupils should be given opportunities to support their work by being taught to:

a find things out from a variety of sources, selecting and synthesising the information to meet their needs and developing an ability to question its accuracy, bias and plausibility

b develop their ideas using ICT tools to amend and refine their work and enhance its quality and accuracy

c exchange and share information, both directly and through electronic media

d review, modify and evaluate their work, reflecting critically on its quality, as it progresses.

[1] At key stage 1, there are no statutory requirements to teach the use of ICT in the programmes of study for the non-core foundation subjects. Teachers should use their judgement to decide where it is appropriate to teach the use of ICT across these subjects at key stage 1. At other key stages, there are statutory requirements to use ICT in all subjects, except physical education.

Health and safety

1   This statement applies to science, design and technology, information and communication technology, art and design, and physical education.

2   When working with tools, equipment and materials, in practical activities and in different environments, including those that are unfamiliar, pupils should be taught:

a   about hazards, risks and risk control

b   to recognise hazards, assess consequent risks and take steps to control the risks to themselves and others

c   to use information to assess the immediate and cumulative risks

d   to manage their environment to ensure the health and safety of themselves and others

e   to explain the steps they take to control risks.

The attainment target
for physical education

About the attainment target

An attainment target sets out the 'knowledge, skills and understanding that pupils of different abilities and maturities are expected to have by the end of each key stage'[1]. Except in the case of citizenship[2], attainment targets consist of eight level descriptions of increasing difficulty, plus a description for exceptional performance above level 8. Each level description describes the types and range of performance that pupils working at that level should characteristically demonstrate.

The level descriptions provide the basis for making judgements about pupils' performance at the end of key stages 1, 2 and 3. At key stage 4, national qualifications are one means of assessing attainment in physical education.

Range of levels within which the great majority of pupils are expected to work		Expected attainment for the majority of pupils at the end of the key stage	
Key stage 1	1–3	at age 7	2
Key stage 2	2–5	at age 11	4
Key stage 3	3–7	at age 14	5/6[3]

Assessing attainment at the end of a key stage

In deciding on a pupil's level of attainment at the end of a key stage, teachers should judge which description best fits the pupil's performance. When doing so, each description should be considered alongside descriptions for adjacent levels.

Arrangements for statutory assessment at the end of each key stage are set out in detail in QCA's annual booklets about assessment and reporting arrangements.

[1] As defined by the Education Act 1996, section 353a.
[2] In citizenship, expected performance for the majority of pupils at the end of key stages 3 and 4 is set out in end of key stage descriptions.
[3] Including modern foreign languages.

Level 5

Pupils select and combine their skills, techniques and ideas and apply them accurately and appropriately, consistently showing precision, control and fluency. When performing, they draw on what they know about strategy, tactics and composition. They analyse and comment on skills and techniques and how these are applied in their own and others' work. They modify and refine skills and techniques to improve their performance. They explain how the body reacts during different types of exercise, and warm up and cool down in ways that suit the activity. They explain why regular, safe exercise is good for their fitness and health.

Level 6

Pupils select and combine skills, techniques and ideas. They apply them in ways that suit the activity, with consistent precision, control and fluency. When planning their own and others' work, and carrying out their own work, they draw on what they know about strategy, tactics and composition in response to changing circumstances, and what they know about their own and others' strengths and weaknesses. They analyse and comment on how skills, techniques and ideas have been used in their own and others' work, and on compositional and other aspects of performance, and suggest ways to improve. They explain how to prepare for, and recover from, the activities. They explain how different types of exercise contribute to their fitness and health and describe how they might get involved in other types of activities and exercise.

Level 7

Pupils select and combine advanced skills, techniques and ideas, adapting them accurately and appropriately to the demands of the activities. They consistently show precision, control, fluency and originality. Drawing on what they know of the principles of advanced tactics and compositional ideas, they apply these in their own and others' work. They modify them in response to changing circumstances and other performers. They analyse and comment on their own and others' work as individuals and team members, showing that they understand how skills, tactics or composition and fitness relate to the quality of the performance. They plan ways to improve their own and others' performance. They explain the principles of practice and training, and apply them effectively. They explain the benefits of regular, planned activity on health and fitness and plan their own appropriate exercise and activity programme.

Level 8

Pupils consistently distinguish and apply advanced skills, techniques and ideas, consistently showing high standards of precision, control, fluency and originality. Drawing on what they know of the principles of advanced tactics or composition, they apply these principles with proficiency and flair in their own and others' work. They adapt it appropriately in response to changing circumstances and other performers. They evaluate their own and others' work, showing that they understand the impact of skills, strategy and tactics or composition, and fitness on the quality and effectiveness of performance. They plan ways in which their own and others' performance could be improved. They create action plans and ways of monitoring improvement. They use their knowledge of health and fitness to plan and evaluate their own and others' exercise and activity programme.

Exceptional performance

Pupils consistently use advanced skills, techniques and ideas with precision and fluency. Drawing on what they know of the principles of advanced strategies and tactics or composition, they consistently apply these principles with originality, proficiency and flair in their own and others' work. They evaluate their own and others' work, showing that they understand how skills, strategy and tactics or composition, and fitness relate to and affect the quality and originality of performance. They reach judgements independently about how their own and others' performance could be improved, prioritising aspects for further development. They consistently apply appropriate knowledge and understanding of health and fitness in all aspects of their work.

Attainment target for physical education

Level 1

Pupils copy, repeat and explore simple skills and actions with basic control and coordination. They start to link these skills and actions in ways that suit the activities. They describe and comment on their own and others' actions. They talk about how to exercise safely, and how their bodies feel during an activity.

Level 2

Pupils explore simple skills. They copy, remember, repeat and explore simple actions with control and coordination. They vary skills, actions and ideas and link these in ways that suit the activities. They begin to show some understanding of simple tactics and basic compositional ideas. They talk about differences between their own and others' performance and suggest improvements. They understand how to exercise safely, and describe how their bodies feel during different activities.

Level 3

Pupils select and use skills, actions and ideas appropriately, applying them with coordination and control. They show that they understand tactics and composition by starting to vary how they respond. They can see how their work is similar to and different from others' work, and use this understanding to improve their own performance. They give reasons why warming up before an activity is important, and why physical activity is good for their health.

Level 4

Pupils link skills, techniques and ideas and apply them accurately and appropriately. Their performance shows precision, control and fluency, and that they understand tactics and composition. They compare and comment on skills, techniques and ideas used in their own and others' work, and use this understanding to improve their performance. They explain and apply basic safety principles in preparing for exercise. They describe what effects exercise has on their bodies, and how it is valuable to their fitness and health.

Acknowledgements

About the work used in this document
The artwork and photographs used in this book are the result of a national selection organised by QCA and the Design Council. We would like to thank all 3,108 pupils who took part and especially the following pupils and schools whose work has been used throughout the National Curriculum.

Pupils Frankie Allen, Sarah Anderson, Naomi Ball, Kristina Battleday, Ashley Boyle, Martin Broom, Katie Brown, Alex Bryant, Tania Burnett, Elizabeth Burrows, Caitie Calloway, Kavandeep Chahal, Donna Clarke, Leah Cliffe, Megan Coombs, Andrew Cornford, Samantha Davidoff, Jodie Evans, Holly Fowler, Rachel Fort, Christopher Fort, Hannah Foster, Ruth Fry, Nicholas Furlonge, Tasleem Ghanchi, Rebecca Goodwin, Megan Goodwin, Joanna Gray, Alisha Grazette, Emma Habbeshon, Zoe Hall, Kay Hampshire, Jessica Harris, Aimee Howard, Amy Hurst, Katherine Hymers, Safwan Ismael, Tamaszina Jacobs-Abiola, Tomi Johnson, Richard Jones, Bruno Jones, Thomas Kelleher, Sophie Lambert, Gareth Lloyd, Ope Majekodunmi, Sophie Manchester, Alex Massie, Amy McNair, Dale Meachen, Katherine Mills, Rebecca Moore, Andrew Morgan, Amber Murrell, Sally O'Connor, Rosie O'Reilly, Antonia Pain, Daniel Pamment, Jennie Plant, Christopher Prest, Megan Ramsay, Alice Ross, David Rowles, Amy Sandford, Zeba Saudagar, Nathan Scarfe, Daniel Scully, Bilal Shakoor, Sandeep Sharma, Morrad Siyahla, Daryl Smith, Catriona Statham, Scott Taylor, Amy Thornton, Jessica Tidmarsh, Alix Tinkler, Lucy Titford, Marion Tulloch, Charlotte Ward, Kaltuun Warsame, Emily Webb, Bradley West, Daniel Wilkinson, Soriah Williams, Susan Williamson, Helen Williamson, Charlotte Windmill, Ryan Wollan, Olivia Wright.

Schools Adam's Grammar School, Almondbury Junior School, Bishops Castle Community College, Bolton Brow Junior and Infant School, Boxford C of E Voluntary Controlled Primary School, Bugbrooke School, Cantell School, Charnwood Primary School, Cheselbourne County First School, Chester Catholic High School, Dales Infant School, Deanery C of E High School, Driffield C of E Infants' School, Dursley Primary School, Fourfields County Primary School, Furze Infants School, Gosforth High School, Grahame Park Junior School, Green Park Combined School, Gusford Community Primary School, Hartshill School, Headington School, Holyport Manor School, Jersey College for Girls Preparatory School, King Edward VI School, King James's School, Kingsway Junior School, Knutsford High School, Leiston Primary School, Maltby Manor Infant School, Mullion Comprehensive School, North Marston C of E First School, Norton Hill School, Penglais School, Priory Secondary School, Redknock School, Richard Whittington Primary School, Ringwood School, Sarah Bonnell School, Sedgemoor Manor Infants School, Selly Park Technology College for Girls, Southwark Infant School, St Albans High School for Girls, St Denys C of E Infant School, St Helen's C of E (Aided) Primary School, St John's Infants School, St Joseph's RC Infant School, St Laurence School, St Mary Magdalene School, St Matthews C of E Aided Primary School, St Michael's C of E School, St Saviour's and St Olave's School, St Thomas The Martyr C of E Primary School, Sawtry Community College, The Duchess's High School, Tideway School, Torfield School, Trinity C of E Primary School, Upper Poppelton School, Walton High School.

QCA and the Design Council would also like to thank the figures from public life who contributed their ideas about the value of each curriculum subject.